Unlikely Heroes: Journeys from Adversity to Triumph
From Broke to Billionaire
By Kevin James Joseph McNamara

performance, effectiveness or applicability of any sites listed or linked to in this eBook. All links are for information purposes only and are not warranted for content, accuracy or any other implied or explicit purpose.

Table Of Contents:

Prologue

Epilogue

Prologue

To those who stand at the precipice of dreams, armed with little more than will and perseverance:

This is for you—the dreamers, the undeterred, the steadfast hearts who have felt the weight of empty pockets and the sting of doors unopened. You are the inheritors of a legacy not of wealth, but of a wealth of possibility.

Within these pages lies not just a chronicle of those who have risen, but a mirror reflecting the potential that resides in the unlikeliest of places—in the quiet moments before dawn, in the silent prayers that accompany the turning of a key in a lock that has yet to yield.

Let each story be a beacon, for they began where you stand now. They were not born atop mountains but rose from valleys deep and forged paths through unyielding stone with tenacity as their compass. They stumbled, they faltered, but they pressed onward, with the glimmer of hope as their guide and the resilience that is the hallmark of every great journey.

So to you, I say: Let the magnitude of their heights make your starting point all the more powerful. Let their legacies be your inspiration, but not your boundaries. For your story is yet unwritten, and the world awaits the mark of your unique passage.

With each step you take, know that the depth of your struggle can be the height of your triumph. Begin with courage, endure with purpose, and prevail with the unwavering belief that the dawn of your legacy is but a persistent heartbeat away.

~ ~ ~ ~ ~

1 - Andrew Carnegie:

Andrew Carnegie's journey from a poor immigrant to one of the most successful industrialists and philanthropists in American history is a testament to the power of determination, innovation, and a deep-rooted belief in the American Dream. His life story is not just a biography of remarkable achievements but also a blueprint for those seeking to overcome obstacles and make a meaningful impact in the world.

Born in Dunfermline, Scotland, in 1835, Carnegie's early life was marked by hardship. His family lived in a small, one-room cottage, and his father, a handloom weaver, struggled to provide for them as the Industrial Revolution rendered his skills obsolete. The Carnegie family's decision to emigrate to the United States in 1848 was driven by the hope of a better life, a decision that would set young Andrew on the path to unparalleled success.

Arriving in Allegheny, Pennsylvania, Carnegie's first job at the age of 13 was as a bobbin boy in a cotton mill, earning a meager $1.20 per week. This early exposure to the harsh realities of labor would later influence his philanthropic efforts towards education and the betterment of the working class. His voracious appetite for learning was evident from a young age, and despite his limited formal education, Carnegie took advantage of every opportunity to educate himself, particularly through reading.

Carnegie's turning point came when he became a telegraph messenger boy and, later, an operator. This position not only honed his communication skills but also introduced him to influential figures such as Thomas A. Scott of the Pennsylvania Railroad, who later employed Carnegie as his personal secretary and telegraph operator. This mentorship was crucial, as Scott provided Carnegie with valuable insights into business and investment.

The outbreak of the Civil War further accelerated Carnegie's rise. His management of the railroads' telegraph lines and his investments in ironworks and bridges that supported the Union war effort laid the foundation for his future in the steel industry. Carnegie's vision of an integrated steel operation led to the formation of the Carnegie Steel Company, which eventually dominated the American steel industry.

Carnegie's business acumen was evident in his adoption of the Bessemer process, which revolutionized steel production by making it more efficient and cost-effective. He also understood the importance of vertical integration, controlling every aspect of the production process, from raw materials to distribution. These strategic decisions not only maximized profits but also allowed Carnegie Steel to undercut competitors and gain a significant market share.

However, Carnegie's legacy is not solely defined by his industrial achievements. His belief in the "Gospel of Wealth" – the idea that the wealthy have a moral obligation to distribute their wealth in ways that promote the welfare and happiness of the common man – shaped his philanthropic endeavors. Carnegie's contributions to public libraries, education, and scientific research were driven by his conviction that access to knowledge was the key to empowering individuals and improving society.

The sale of Carnegie Steel to J.P. Morgan in 1901, which formed U.S. Steel, marked Carnegie's retirement from business and his full-time dedication to philanthropy. He gave away over $350 million (equivalent to billions today) to various causes, a sum that was unprecedented at the time.

Carnegie's life offers several lessons for those aspiring to overcome obstacles and achieve success. Firstly, the importance of education and self-improvement cannot be overstated. Carnegie's commitment to learning, despite his limited formal education, was a key factor in his rise. Secondly, the value of mentorship and networking is evident in Carnegie's relationship with Thomas A. Scott and other influential figures. Thirdly, Carnegie's strategic thinking and innovation in business highlight the importance of adapting to change and seizing opportunities. Finally, his philanthropic philosophy underscores the responsibility that comes with wealth and success.

In conclusion, Andrew Carnegie's story is a powerful illustration of how determination, innovation, and a commitment to the greater good can lead to extraordinary achievements. His legacy serves as a beacon for those navigating the challenges of life and striving to make a positive impact in the world.

2 - Berry Gordy:

In the rhythm of American history, few beats have resonated as powerfully as the Motown sound, orchestrated by the visionary Berry Gordy. His story is a symphony of ambition, creativity, and resilience, echoing the cultural movements of his time and harmonizing personal triumph with societal progress.

Born in Detroit in 1929, Gordy's early life was set against the backdrop of the Great Depression and the pulsating energy of a city known for its automotive industry. The son of a plastering contractor and a schoolteacher, Gordy's upbringing was steeped in a strong work ethic and an appreciation for education. However, it was his love for music, kindled by his family's frequent singalongs, that would eventually chart the course of his life.

Gordy's initial foray into the music industry was as a songwriter, but his ambitions extended beyond penning lyrics. He envisioned a record label that would not only produce hit records but also nurture African American talent and break down racial barriers in the music industry. This dream led to the birth of Motown Records in 1959, a venture that started with an $800 loan from his family's savings.

Establishing Motown was a challenge that required Gordy to wear multiple hats: producer, songwriter, talent scout, and businessman. He transformed a modest house on West Grand Boulevard, famously known as "Hitsville USA," into a music-making powerhouse. Gordy's keen ear for talent brought artists like Smokey Robinson, Diana Ross, Stevie Wonder, and Marvin Gaye under the Motown umbrella, creating a family-like atmosphere that fostered creativity and camaraderie.

The early days of Motown were marked by a relentless pursuit of success in an industry that was often unwelcoming to Black artists and entrepreneurs. Gordy's determination to break through these barriers was fueled by a unique approach to music production. He combined the catchy rhythms of R&B with the polished appeal of pop, creating a sound that transcended racial boundaries and appealed to a broad audience. This "Motown Sound" became a symbol of racial integration in a time of segregation, bridging divides not only in music but also in society.

Gordy's innovative strategies extended beyond the music itself. He established a rigorous artist development program, grooming his artists for mainstream success by teaching them everything from stage presence to etiquette. This meticulous attention to detail ensured that Motown artists could captivate audiences of all backgrounds, making them ambassadors of a new, inclusive musical era.

The impact of Motown under Gordy's leadership was profound. The label produced an astounding number of hits, shaping the soundtrack of the 1960s and 70s and leaving an indelible mark on the cultural landscape. Motown's success demonstrated the commercial viability of Black music and paved the way for future generations of African American artists and entrepreneurs.

The lessons from Berry Gordy's journey are as timeless as the music he helped create. His story teaches us the power of vision and perseverance in the face of adversity. It highlights the importance of adaptability and innovation in achieving success. Gordy's commitment to breaking down racial barriers reminds us of the role that art and culture can play in fostering social change.

In the melody of Berry Gordy's life, we find inspiration to pursue our passions, to challenge the status quo, and to build bridges that unite us. His legacy, like the Motown sound, continues to resonate, encouraging us to dream big and to create our own harmonies in the symphony of life.

3 - Chris Gardner:

I'm Chris Gardner, and my journey from homelessness to becoming a successful entrepreneur is a testament to the power of persistence and resilience. It's a story that proves no matter how hard life hits, you can always fight your way back to the top.

My early years were far from easy. I grew up in Milwaukee, Wisconsin, under the care of my mother, Bettye Jean. She was a beacon of strength and hope, teaching me the importance of self-reliance and education. Despite her efforts, life threw curveballs at us. My stepfather was abusive, and we often found ourselves in volatile situations. I learned early on that if I wanted a different life, I'd have to carve it out myself.

I joined the Navy, hoping it would be my ticket to a better future. After my discharge, I moved to San Francisco, driven by the dream of making it big in medicine. I became a medical equipment salesman, a job that introduced me to the world of finance. It was during a sales call that I met a stockbroker who drove a red Ferrari. That encounter sparked a new dream in me - I wanted to be a stockbroker.

But life has a way of testing your resolve. Just as I was trying to break into the world of finance, my personal life began to crumble. My relationship with my girlfriend fell apart, and she left, taking our son, Christopher, with her. I was devastated. When she returned months later, I gained custody of our son, determined to give him a stable life.

The path to becoming a stockbroker was riddled with obstacles. I managed to land a spot in a training program, but there was a catch - it was unpaid. With no steady income, paying rent became impossible. Before I knew it, Christopher and I were homeless.

Imagine trying to learn the intricacies of finance while not knowing where you're going to sleep at night. I'd leave Christopher at daycare, spend my day at work, then pick him up, and we'd search for a place to stay. We slept in shelters, parks, and even public restrooms. It was a time of profound despair, but I refused to give up. I knew I had to keep pushing for my son's sake and mine.

Every day, I'd put on my suit, hiding the fact that I was homeless from my colleagues. I studied hard, aced my exams, and finally landed a job as a stockbroker. From there, things started looking up. I worked tirelessly, building my client base and reputation in the industry.

Looking back, the lessons I learned during those challenging times are invaluable. Resilience is not just about surviving; it's about thriving despite the odds. It's about holding onto your dreams, even when they seem impossible. Persistence is key. No matter how many times you get knocked down, you've got to get back up and keep moving forward.

My story is a reminder that your current circumstances don't define your future. With determination and a relentless spirit, you can overcome any obstacle. It's a message I've shared through my book, "The Pursuit of Happyness," and it's a message I'll continue to share as long as I can. Life is a journey of ups and downs, but with perseverance, you can turn your lowest points into the foundation of your greatest successes.

4 - Colonel Harland Sanders:

Colonel Harland Sanders' story is a classic tale of American grit and determination, seasoned with a dash of Southern charm. His journey to founding Kentucky Fried Chicken (KFC) is a testament to the idea that it's never too late to find success, challenging the common belief that achievement has an expiration date.

Born in 1890 in Henryville, Indiana, Sanders' early life was anything but easy. After losing his father at a young age, he was thrust into the role of caretaker for his siblings while his mother worked long hours. This meant learning to cook, a skill that would later define his legacy. Despite his responsibilities, Sanders was a restless spirit, trying his hand at various jobs, from farmhand to streetcar conductor.

His foray into the culinary world began in earnest when he started running a service station in Corbin, Kentucky, in the 1930s. Here, he began serving home-cooked meals to travelers, and it wasn't long before his fried chicken gained a reputation. But success was not immediate. Sanders spent years perfecting his recipe, facing rejection after rejection as he tried to franchise his chicken. It wasn't until he was in his sixties, an age when many would consider retirement, that his efforts began to pay off.

The turning point came when Sanders developed his secret recipe of 11 herbs and spices, and his unique method of pressure frying chicken, which kept it juicy while ensuring a crispy exterior. This culinary innovation set his chicken apart and became the cornerstone of KFC's success. But it wasn't just his recipe that made Sanders a household name; it was his tireless work ethic and refusal to give up, even in the face of repeated failures.

Sanders' late-life success with KFC challenges the common belief that success is reserved for the young. His story is a reminder that passion and perseverance have no age limit. He didn't let societal norms dictate the timing of his achievements, proving that it's never too late to pursue your dreams.

The lessons from Colonel Sanders' life are as hearty and wholesome as his famous chicken. He showed that success is not just about having a great idea, but also about the dedication to see it through, regardless of the obstacles. His journey teaches us the value of resilience, the importance of believing in your vision, and the power of hard work.

In the end, Colonel Harland Sanders' legacy is not just about the finger-lickin' good chicken he created. It's about the spirit of American entrepreneurship and the belief that with enough grit and determination, anyone can achieve their dreams, no matter their age. His story serves as a hearty helping of inspiration for anyone who thinks their time has passed. In the words of Sanders himself, "One has to remember that every failure can be a stepping stone to something better."

5 - Dhirubhai Ambani:

Dhirubhai Ambani's story is a riveting saga of a visionary who emerged from the depths of poverty to become a titan of the Indian business world. His life is a testament to the power of ambition, strategic foresight, and an unyielding belief in the potential of India's economy.

Born in 1932 in a small village in Gujarat, Ambani's early life was marked by financial hardship. His father was a schoolteacher, and the family struggled to make ends meet. Despite these challenges, Ambani harbored big dreams. He understood from a young age that to achieve something extraordinary, one must dare to dream big and take risks.

Ambani's journey to success began in the bustling lanes of Mumbai, where he moved in his late teens. He started his career working as a clerk for a trading company, where he learned the ropes of the trading business. But Ambani was not content with a life of mediocrity. He had a keen eye for opportunities and a mind that was constantly strategizing for the future.

In 1958, with a modest capital, he took his first step into entrepreneurship by starting a trading business dealing in spices and textiles. His business acumen and relentless work ethic quickly set him apart. He understood the importance of customer satisfaction and built a reputation for delivering quality products at competitive prices.

However, it was his foray into the textile industry that marked the beginning of his meteoric rise. Ambani's strategic foresight led him to recognize the potential of synthetic fabrics in India. In 1966, he established Reliance Textiles, introducing the brand 'Vimal,' which became synonymous with quality and affordability. His innovative marketing strategies, such as franchising retail outlets and aggressive advertising, revolutionized the textile industry in India.

Ambani's vision extended beyond textiles. He saw the potential for growth in diverse sectors and ventured into petrochemicals, telecommunications, and information technology. Each of these ventures was guided by his belief in the power of the Indian market and his ability to foresee global trends.

One of Ambani's most significant contributions to the Indian business landscape was his democratization of the stock market. He made it possible for millions of middle-class Indians to invest in shares, thereby broadening the base of the Indian stock market. His ability to raise capital from the public transformed the way businesses were funded in India.

Ambani's risk-taking appetite was legendary. He often ventured into uncharted territories, betting on the future with a conviction that was rare. His success was not without challenges. He faced criticism, legal battles, and intense competition, but his determination and belief in his vision were unwavering.

The legacy of Dhirubhai Ambani is not just the conglomerate Reliance Industries, which stands as a testament to his entrepreneurial genius. His legacy is the belief that with ambition, strategic foresight, and a willingness to take risks, anyone can transcend their circumstances and achieve greatness.

Ambani's story offers several lessons for aspiring entrepreneurs. It highlights the importance of having a vision and the courage to pursue it relentlessly. It underscores the value of innovation, customer focus, and the ability to adapt to changing market dynamics. Above all, it demonstrates that with determination and strategic thinking, even the most ambitious dreams can be realized.

In conclusion, Dhirubhai Ambani's saga is a beacon of inspiration for anyone looking to make their mark in the world of business. His journey from rags to riches, driven by strategic foresight and ambition, transformed the Indian business landscape and serves as a powerful reminder that it's not where you start but where you're willing to go that truly matters.

6 - Do Won Chang and Jin Sook Chang:

Do Won Chang and Jin Sook Chang's story is a quintessential immigrant tale of hard work, family teamwork, and the relentless pursuit of the American dream. Their journey from South Korea to the founders of the global retail giant Forever 21 is a testament to the possibilities that lie in the vast expanse of the American retail landscape.

The Changs' journey began in the 1980s when they moved to the United States from South Korea in search of better opportunities. Like many immigrants, they arrived with limited resources and faced the daunting challenge of building a new life in a foreign land. The language barrier and cultural differences added to their struggles, but the Changs were determined to succeed.

Do Won initially worked as a janitor, while Jin Sook was employed as a hairdresser. They saved every penny, living frugally and dreaming of a better future. The turning point came when they recognized a gap in the American retail market for affordable, trendy clothing. With their savings and a small loan, they opened their first clothing store in 1984, named Fashion 21, in Los Angeles.

The store was a modest 900-square-foot space, but the Changs' unique approach to retail quickly set them apart. They focused on fast fashion, rapidly changing their inventory to keep up with the latest trends. This strategy, coupled with affordable prices, struck a chord with young, fashion-conscious customers. The store's success was immediate, and within a year, they were able to open a second location.

The Changs' success was built on more than just a keen understanding of the market. It was their teamwork and family-oriented approach that were the bedrock of their business. They involved their children in the business from a young age, instilling in them the values of hard work and dedication. The family worked tirelessly, often putting in long hours to ensure the success of their stores.

As the business grew, the Changs rebranded their stores to Forever 21, reflecting their desire to cater to a demographic that wanted to stay forever young and fashionable. The brand expanded rapidly, both nationally and internationally, becoming a household name in the fast-fashion industry.

The Changs' journey was not without its challenges. The fast-paced growth of Forever 21 led to logistical and operational hurdles. They faced criticism over labor practices and the environmental impact of fast fashion. Yet, they continued to adapt and evolve, addressing these issues and striving to improve their business practices.

The story of Do Won and Jin Sook Chang is a powerful example of immigrant entrepreneurship. It highlights the challenges faced by immigrants in navigating a new country and the retail industry's competitive landscape. It also showcases the triumphs that can be achieved through perseverance, teamwork, and a clear vision.

Their journey provides several key lessons for aspiring entrepreneurs. It underscores the importance of identifying market opportunities and being agile in responding to consumer trends. It emphasizes the value of hard work, family support, and maintaining a strong team ethos. Most importantly, it demonstrates that with determination and a willingness to take risks, success is within reach, regardless of one's background.

In conclusion, the Changs' story is a reminder that the American dream is alive and well for those who are willing to pursue it with passion and persistence. Their legacy in the retail industry and their impact on the fast-fashion world continue to inspire entrepreneurs around the globe, proving that with the right mindset and support, anything is possible.

7 - Francois Pinault:

François Pinault's odyssey from a modest background in rural Brittany to the pinnacle of the global luxury and art world is a dramatic narrative of resilience, vision, and an unyielding desire to transcend conventional boundaries. His journey is a testament to the idea that even the most unconventional paths can lead to extraordinary achievements in the realms of high fashion and art patronage.

Born in 1936 in the small town of Les Champs-Géraux, Pinault's early life was far removed from the glamour of the luxury industry. His family was working-class, and he grew up in a world where hard work was a necessity rather than a choice. Despite the humble beginnings, Pinault harbored ambitions that stretched beyond the confines of his provincial upbringing.

Pinault's academic journey was marked by challenges. He struggled with dyslexia, a condition that made traditional learning difficult and eventually led him to drop out of school at the age of 16. However, this setback did not deter him. Instead, it fueled his determination to succeed on his own terms. He embarked on a career in the timber industry, a decision that laid the groundwork for his future empire.

The turning point in Pinault's career came in the 1960s when he took a bold step to start his own business, Établissements Pinault, a wood and building materials company. This venture marked the beginning of his foray into the business world, and his entrepreneurial spirit quickly set him apart. Pinault's keen eye for opportunity and his willingness to take risks propelled his business to new heights.

As his business acumen grew, so did his ambitions. In the 1980s and 1990s, Pinault shifted his focus from the timber trade to the retail and luxury sectors. His acquisition of the bankrupt department store Printemps and the subsequent investments in high-end brands such as Château Latour, Gucci, and Yves Saint Laurent, among others, were strategic moves that redefined his business trajectory. These acquisitions were not merely financial investments; they were a reflection of Pinault's deep appreciation for craftsmanship, quality, and the art of luxury.

Pinault's unconventional path to success was also mirrored in his approach to building his luxury empire. He was not content with merely owning prestigious brands; he wanted to elevate them to new heights of excellence and innovation. His hands-on involvement and respect for the creative process endeared him to the fashion world, and under his stewardship, brands like Gucci flourished, setting new standards in the industry.

Beyond the world of fashion, Pinault emerged as a significant patron of the arts. His personal art collection, featuring works by the likes of Picasso, Mondrian, and Koons, is among the most impressive in the world. His commitment to art culminated in the establishment of the Pinault Collection, housed in two iconic venues in Venice and the Bourse de Commerce in Paris. Through these endeavors, Pinault has not only showcased his passion for art but also contributed to the cultural landscape, making art accessible to a wider audience.

François Pinault's journey offers a wealth of lessons for those aspiring to carve their own paths. His story demonstrates that formal education is not the only route to success; determination and a willingness to learn from experience can be equally powerful. It highlights the importance of being adaptable and seizing opportunities, even when they deviate from conventional norms. Moreover, Pinault's life underscores the value of passion, whether in the pursuit of business excellence or the appreciation of art.

In conclusion, François Pinault's ascent from a school dropout to a titan of the luxury and art worlds is a sophisticated tale of ambition, innovation, and an unwavering belief in the beauty of the unconventional. His legacy is a reminder that the path to success is not always linear, and that with vision and perseverance, even the most humble beginnings can lead to the heights of high fashion and art patronage.

8 - George Soros:

George Soros' life is a tapestry of survival, intellect, and a deep understanding of the world's financial and historical complexities. Born in 1930 in Budapest, Hungary, to a Jewish family, Soros' early years were marked by the ominous shadows of Nazism and later, Communism. These experiences not only tested his will to survive but also shaped his world view, financial acumen, and philanthropic vision.

Surviving the Nazi occupation of Hungary during World War II was Soros' first encounter with the brutal realities of political turmoil and persecution. His father, Tivadar Soros, a lawyer and an esperantist, used his wit and resources to forge documents that saved his family from the Holocaust. This period of extreme adversity ingrained in

Soros a sense of danger, but also the importance of being adaptive and resourceful.

Post-war Hungary offered little respite, as the country fell under Communist rule. Soros' encounter with these oppressive regimes early in life fostered in him a deep-seated aversion to authoritarianism and a belief in the power of individual freedom. In 1947, seizing an opportunity to escape the Communist grip, Soros emigrated to England, where he attended the London School of Economics (LSE).

At LSE, Soros was influenced by the philosopher Karl Popper, who became a lifelong mentor. Popper's concept of the "open society" – a society where individual rights are respected, and government is accountable – resonated deeply with Soros. This philosophy would later become the cornerstone of his philanthropic efforts.

Soros' entry into the world of finance began at a London merchant bank, followed by stints at various financial institutions in the United States. His understanding of markets and economies was not just theoretical; it was also intuitive. Soros had an uncanny ability to discern the dynamic interplay between economic, political, and social forces. This holistic approach to finance was evident in his establishment of the Quantum Fund in 1973, a hedge fund that would become the vehicle for his legendary financial success.

One of Soros' most notable financial maneuvers was his bet against the British pound in 1992, a move that earned him the moniker "the man who broke the Bank of England." His decision to short the pound was based on a deep understanding of the political and economic forces at play, showcasing his ability to turn complex analyses into profitable strategies. This event not only solidified his reputation as a financial wizard but also demonstrated his belief in acting on convictions, even when they go against the tide.

Soros' financial success is paralleled by his philanthropic endeavors. In 1979, he founded the Open Society Foundations, a network of foundations dedicated to promoting democracy, human rights, and social justice across the globe. His commitment to these causes stems from his own experiences of living through totalitarian regimes and his conviction that societies can only thrive when they are open and free.

Through his philanthropy, Soros has supported a wide range of initiatives, from education and public health to political reform and civil society building. His approach to philanthropy is reflective of his financial strategies – bold, unconventional, and often ahead of the curve. Soros has not shied away from supporting causes that are controversial but align with his vision of an open society.

The story of George Soros is a complex narrative of survival, financial acumen, and a commitment to a better world. His life's journey offers several lessons. It underscores the importance of resilience in the face of adversity, the value of a well-rounded understanding of the world, and the power of conviction-driven action. Soros' legacy is a reminder that one's experiences, no matter how challenging, can be a catalyst for profound impact on both the financial markets and society at large.

9 - Guy Laliberté:

Guy Laliberté's journey from a street performer in Quebec to the mastermind behind Cirque du Soleil is a vibrant tapestry woven with threads of creativity, innovation, and an unwavering belief in the magic of the circus. His story is a testament to the power of imagination and the limitless potential of the human spirit to redefine entertainment for modern audiences.

Laliberté's early life was filled with the colors of creativity and the desire for adventure. Born in 1959 in Quebec City, he was a curious and spirited child, always seeking new ways to express himself. His journey into the world of performance began with a passion for the accordion, stilt-walking, and fire-breathing, skills that would later become the foundation of his entertainment empire.

In the late 1970s, Laliberté took to the streets, performing with a group of like-minded artists who shared his passion for bringing joy and wonder to the public. These early experiences as a street performer taught him valuable lessons in engaging audiences and the importance of creating a unique and memorable experience. It was during this time that he honed his skills and developed his vision for a new kind of circus.

The turning point in Laliberté's career came in 1984 when he co-founded Cirque du Soleil with a small government grant intended to celebrate the 450th anniversary of Jacques Cartier's discovery of Canada. With limited resources and a bold vision, Laliberté set out to create a circus that was unlike anything the world had ever seen. He envisioned a show that combined the artistry of street performance with the grandeur of the circus, creating a unique blend of music, dance, acrobatics, and visual spectacle.

Cirque du Soleil's first show, "Le Grand Tour du Cirque du Soleil," was a modest success, but it laid the groundwork for what would become a global entertainment phenomenon. Laliberté's creativity and innovation were evident in every aspect of the production, from the elimination of animal acts to the incorporation of elaborate costumes, original music, and stunning acrobatic feats. His approach to circus entertainment was revolutionary, transforming the traditional circus into a sophisticated, artistic performance that appealed to a broader, adult audience.

The success of Cirque du Soleil grew exponentially with each new show, and Laliberté's vision continued to evolve. He pushed the boundaries of performance art, constantly seeking new ways to captivate audiences and create unforgettable experiences. His dedication to innovation and excellence propelled Cirque du Soleil to international fame, with shows performed in over 300 cities on six continents.

Laliberté's journey is a vivid illustration of the creativity and innovation required to reinvent the circus for modern audiences. His story teaches us the importance of following our passions, thinking outside the box, and the transformative power of art and entertainment. It is a reminder that with imagination and perseverance, even the most unconventional ideas can become a reality.

In conclusion, Guy Laliberté's transformation from a street performer to the creator of Cirque du Soleil is a colorful and imaginative narrative that mirrors the creativity of his productions. His legacy is not only the global entertainment phenomenon he created but also the inspiration he provides to dreamers and innovators everywhere. His journey is a testament to the fact that with creativity, innovation, and a little bit of magic, anything is possible.

10 - Howard Schultz:

Howard Schultz's ascent from the housing projects of Brooklyn to the helm of Starbucks is a narrative steeped in the themes of social mobility and the desire to create a 'third place' between work and home. His journey is a testament to the power of vision, resilience, and a deep-seated belief in the value of community and corporate social responsibility.

Born in 1953, Schultz grew up in a low-income family in the Canarsie Bayview Houses of Brooklyn, New York. His early life was marked by financial hardship and the challenges that come with growing up in a tough neighborhood. These experiences instilled in him a strong sense of empathy and a desire to create opportunities for people from all walks of life.

Schultz's first encounter with Starbucks was as a sales representative for a Swedish drip coffee maker company. Impressed by the volume of orders from a small coffee shop in Seattle, he decided to pay a visit. It was during this visit that Schultz experienced an epiphany. He saw the potential for Starbucks to become more than just a coffee shop; he envisioned it as a community hub where people could gather, connect, and share experiences.

This vision was deeply influenced by Schultz's trip to Italy, where he observed the integral role of coffee bars in Italian culture. He was fascinated by the idea of a 'third place' - a space that was neither home nor work, where people could enjoy a sense of belonging and community. Schultz saw this as an opportunity to recreate a similar experience in America, where such a place was lacking.

In 1987, Schultz acquired Starbucks and set out to transform it into the 'third place' he had envisioned. He focused on creating a welcoming and comfortable environment, where customers could linger over a cup of coffee and engage in conversations. He believed that Starbucks should not just sell coffee, but an experience - one that fostered a sense of community and connection.

Schultz's upbringing played a crucial role in shaping his approach to corporate social responsibility. Growing up in a struggling family, he understood the importance of giving back to the community and providing opportunities for those in need. Under his leadership, Starbucks implemented various social initiatives, including offering health insurance to part-time employees, investing in community service projects, and promoting sustainable and ethical sourcing practices.

Schultz's vision for Starbucks was not just about creating a successful business; it was about creating a positive impact on society. He believed that corporations have a responsibility to contribute to the well-being of the communities they serve. This belief was reflected in Starbucks' mission to inspire and nurture the human spirit - one person, one cup, and one neighborhood at a time.

The story of Howard Schultz is a powerful example of how personal experiences can shape a leader's vision and values. It demonstrates the impact that a socially responsible business can have on society, and the importance of creating spaces that foster community and connection. Schultz's journey from the housing projects of Brooklyn to the CEO of Starbucks is a testament to the possibilities of social mobility and the transformative power of a clear and compassionate vision.

In conclusion, Howard Schultz's narrative is a compelling tale of social mobility and the quest to create a 'third place' between work and home. His upbringing influenced his vision for Starbucks and his approach to corporate social responsibility, resulting in a global brand that is not only a coffee giant but also a community builder. His story offers valuable lessons in leadership, empathy, and the power of a dream rooted in the desire to make a positive difference in the world.

11 - Ingvar Kamprad:

Ingvar Kamprad's journey to creating IKEA, a global furniture empire, is a testament to the principles of simplicity and cost-consciousness. His story is one of pragmatic decisions and a relentless focus on efficiency, mirroring the functional and no-frills approach that IKEA is known for.

Born in 1926 in Småland, Sweden, Kamprad grew up in a region known for its frugality and hardworking people. These early surroundings instilled in him a deep sense of cost-consciousness and an appreciation for making the most of limited resources. From a young age, Kamprad exhibited a knack for business. He started by selling matches to neighbors from his bicycle and quickly expanded to selling fish, Christmas tree decorations, and seeds.

The turning point in Kamprad's entrepreneurial journey came in 1943 when he founded IKEA at the age of 17. The name IKEA is an acronym derived from his initials (I.K.) and the first letters of Elmtaryd and Agunnaryd, the farm and village where he grew up. Initially, IKEA sold small items like pens, wallets, and picture frames. However,

Kamprad's vision was to provide a wide range of home furnishings that were both affordable and well-designed.

Kamprad's principles of simplicity and cost-consciousness were evident in IKEA's early operations. He sought to reduce costs at every turn, from using local manufacturers to flat-packing furniture to save on transport costs. This innovative approach not only lowered prices for customers but also made the furniture easier to transport and assemble at home, embodying the company's focus on functionality.

In 1956, IKEA introduced the concept of flat-packed furniture, a decision that would revolutionize the furniture industry. This idea came about as a practical solution to a problem – a table that couldn't fit into a car. By removing the legs and packing them flat, the table became easier to transport. This simple yet effective solution epitomized Kamprad's philosophy of making life easier for the customer while keeping costs down.

Kamprad's commitment to simplicity extended beyond IKEA's products to its store design and layout. He introduced self-service warehouses and showroom stores, where customers could see and touch the products before making a purchase. This not only improved the shopping experience but also reduced the need for sales staff, further lowering costs.

Under Kamprad's leadership, IKEA expanded rapidly, both in Sweden and internationally. He maintained a hands-on approach to the business, often visiting stores to ensure they adhered to his principles of cost-consciousness and simplicity. Kamprad believed that a well-designed product should be accessible to everyone, not just the wealthy. This democratic approach to design became a core tenet of IKEA's philosophy.

Kamprad's personal life also reflected the values he instilled in IKEA. He was known for his frugal lifestyle, driving an old car and flying economy class, despite his immense wealth. He believed that leading by example was the best way to instill the company's values in his employees.

In conclusion, Ingvar Kamprad's creation of IKEA was driven by his unwavering commitment to simplicity and cost-consciousness. His pragmatic approach to business, focus on functionality, and dedication to making good design accessible to all, have left an indelible mark on the furniture industry. Kamprad's story is a powerful reminder that success can be built on the principles of simplicity and efficiency, and that great things can be achieved by staying true to one's values.

12 – Jack Ma:

"The Unlikely Trailblazer: The Journey of Jack Ma"

In the heart of China's Zhejiang province lies the city of Hangzhou, where the story of a man who would one day revolutionize the global e-commerce landscape began. This is the tale of Jack Ma, a man whose life is a testament to the power of resilience, vision, and relentless pursuit of dreams.

Born on September 10, 1964, into a modest family, Jack Ma was no stranger to hardship. His parents were traditional music-storytellers, and the family struggled to make ends meet. Despite the financial challenges, Jack was an inquisitive child, always eager to learn and explore new horizons.

His journey was marked by early failures and rejections. Jack failed his college entrance exams twice, a setback that would have deterred many. But not Jack. He persevered, eventually gaining admission to Hangzhou Teacher's Institute, where he graduated with a degree in English. This achievement was more than just academic; it was a gateway to the world, as it allowed Jack to interact with foreign visitors, honing his language skills and broadening his perspective.

The early 1990s marked a turning point in Jack's life. During a trip to the United States, he was introduced to the internet, a technology still in its infancy. The idea of a connected world fascinated him, and he saw its potential to transform business and society. Returning to China, he was determined to bring this vision to life. His first venture, China Pages, aimed to create an online directory for Chinese businesses. Though it didn't take off as he hoped, it laid the foundation for what was to come.

In 1999, Jack Ma, along with 18 friends and colleagues, founded Alibaba from his apartment in Hangzhou. The goal was simple yet ambitious: to create a platform that would allow small and medium-sized Chinese businesses to connect with global markets. The road was anything but smooth. The dot-com bubble burst, and the company faced intense competition from established players like eBay. But Jack's unwavering belief in the potential of the internet and e-commerce, coupled with his charismatic leadership, kept the team focused and motivated.

Alibaba's breakthrough came with the introduction of Taobao, a consumer-to-consumer marketplace, and Alipay, a payment platform that addressed the trust gap in online transactions. These innovations not only propelled Alibaba to the forefront of China's e-commerce industry but also laid the groundwork for the company's expansion into various sectors, including cloud computing, digital entertainment, and logistics.

Jack Ma's leadership style is as unconventional as his journey. He emphasizes the importance of culture and values, often drawing from traditional Chinese philosophy and martial arts in his management approach. He believes in leading by example, inspiring his employees to think big and fight for their dreams.

Under his guidance, Alibaba has not just become a commercial success but also a symbol of the possibilities that arise when technology meets human ingenuity. Jack Ma's story is a reminder that the path to success is not always linear. It is filled with obstacles, but with resilience, a clear vision, and a willingness to embrace change, even the most unlikely underdog can leave an indelible mark on the world.

Today, as Jack Ma steps back from his corporate roles to focus on philanthropy and education, his legacy continues to inspire entrepreneurs and dreamers worldwide. His journey from a humble English teacher to a global business magnate is a testament to the fact that with passion and perseverance, anything is possible.

13 - Jan Koum:

Jan Koum's journey from a modest upbringing in Ukraine to co-founding WhatsApp, one of the world's most widely used messaging apps, is a story of resilience, innovation, and the transformative power of technology.

Born in a small village near Kyiv, Ukraine, in 1976, Koum's early life was marked by the challenges of growing up in a Soviet-era apartment with limited resources. His family's apartment lacked basic amenities, and privacy was a luxury they could not afford. This lack of privacy left a lasting impression on Koum, shaping his views on the importance of secure communication.

In 1992, seeking a better life and escaping the political and anti-Semitic turmoil in Ukraine, Koum and his mother immigrated to Mountain View, California. They settled in a modest two-bedroom apartment, relying on government assistance to get by. Koum's mother took up babysitting jobs, while he worked as a cleaner at a local grocery store. Despite these humble beginnings, Koum was determined to make the most of his new life in the United States.

Koum's interest in technology was sparked during his high school years. He taught himself computer networking by purchasing manuals from a used bookstore and returning them after he had finished reading. This self-taught knowledge paved the way for his future success in the tech industry.

After high school, Koum enrolled at San Jose State University, where he studied computer science. To support himself, he worked as a security tester for Ernst & Young. It was during this time that he met Brian Acton, a fellow employee at Ernst & Young, who would later become his co-founder at WhatsApp.

Koum's time at San Jose State University was short-lived, as he dropped out to join Yahoo as an infrastructure engineer. He spent nine years at Yahoo, where he honed his skills in network security and infrastructure development. Despite the financial success and stability his job provided, Koum felt unfulfilled and yearned for something more.

In January 2009, after leaving Yahoo, Koum purchased an iPhone and realized the potential of the then-nascent app industry. He envisioned a messaging app that would not only allow users to communicate but also maintain their privacy. This idea was deeply influenced by his early experiences in Ukraine, where privacy was often compromised.

Koum shared his idea with Acton, and together, they co-founded WhatsApp. The app's name was a play on the phrase "What's Up," reflecting its purpose as a simple and casual messaging tool. WhatsApp's initial version allowed users to update their status, letting friends know what they were up to. However, it was the introduction of the messaging feature that transformed WhatsApp into a global phenomenon.

WhatsApp's growth was exponential, reaching 200 million active users by February 2013. Its success caught the attention of Facebook, which acquired the app for $19 billion in February 2014. This acquisition made Koum a billionaire and solidified his place in the tech industry.

Koum's journey is a testament to the power of determination, innovation, and staying true to one's values. His story inspires aspiring entrepreneurs and tech enthusiasts to pursue their dreams, no matter how humble their beginnings. It also serves as a reminder of the impact that technology can have on communication and privacy in the modern world.

In conclusion, Jan Koum's story is not just about the creation of a successful app; it's about overcoming adversity, embracing opportunities, and the relentless pursuit of a vision that can change the way people connect. His journey from a small village in Ukraine to the heights of Silicon Valley is a testament to the fact that with passion, perseverance, and a clear vision, anything is possible.

14 - John Paul DeJoria:

John Paul DeJoria's ascent from the depths of homelessness to the pinnacle of luxury branding is a remarkable saga of resilience, entrepreneurial acumen, and philanthropic commitment. His life's journey is a vivid illustration that adversity can be the crucible in which character and success are forged, and that true accomplishment encompasses not only personal prosperity but also the betterment of society.

Born into a modest family in Los Angeles in 1944, DeJoria's early years were steeped in financial struggle. The divorce of his parents when he was just two years old marked the beginning of a challenging childhood. By the age of nine, DeJoria was already contributing to his family's income, selling Christmas cards and newspapers. These early experiences were the crucible in which his work ethic and appreciation for the value of money were forged.

The trajectory of DeJoria's life was anything but linear. Following a stint in the Navy, he navigated through a series of odd jobs, from pumping gas to janitorial work. It was during this period that he encountered the harsh reality of homelessness. These experiences of living without a roof over his head were not just periods of hardship but also pivotal moments that shaped his entrepreneurial spirit. They taught him invaluable lessons in resilience, resourcefulness, and the unwavering belief in one's ability to alter their destiny.

Amidst these trials, DeJoria's dreams remained undimmed. In 1980, armed with a modest loan of $700, he co-founded John Paul Mitchell Systems alongside hairdresser Paul Mitchell. This venture marked the inception of a company that would redefine the hair care industry. DeJoria's vision was to create premium, high-quality hair care products that were accessible to both stylists and consumers. His commitment to excellence, coupled with innovative marketing strategies, catapulted the company to success, transforming it into a household name in luxury hair care.

DeJoria's encounters with homelessness profoundly influenced his business philosophy and philanthropic endeavors. Having experienced life on the fringes of society, he developed a deep sense of empathy for those struggling to make ends meet. This empathy was reflected in his business practices, such as his commitment to ensuring that his products were never tested on animals and his advocacy for environmental sustainability.

Furthermore, DeJoria's dedication to giving back is evident in his numerous philanthropic initiatives. He has supported a wide array of causes, from funding mobile medical clinics for the homeless to supporting veterans and environmental conservation. His belief in the power of social responsibility has been a guiding force in his life, motivating him to use his success as a means to effect positive change in the world.

DeJoria's journey from homelessness to the helm of a luxury brand empire is a testament to the fact that our past does not dictate our future. His story is a powerful beacon of hope for aspiring entrepreneurs and anyone facing adversity, demonstrating that with determination, a strong work ethic, and a compassionate heart, it is possible to surmount even the most formidable challenges. His life serves as an inspiration, showing that success is not merely about amassing wealth, but also about leveraging that wealth to create a better world for others.

In conclusion, John Paul DeJoria's narrative is not just a tale of personal triumph; it is a story of transformation, from a life of hardship to one of luxury branding and philanthropy. His journey underscores the importance of perseverance, the value of empathy, and the impact of social responsibility. It is a reminder that true success is measured not by what we acquire for ourselves, but by what we contribute to the lives of others. DeJoria's legacy is a testament to the enduring power of hope and the boundless potential of the human spirit to transcend adversity and make a lasting difference in the world.

15 - Kirk Kerkorian:

Kirk Kerkorian's odyssey through the dazzling world of Las Vegas is a high-stakes narrative of ambition, strategic acumen, and the art of the deal. His journey from humble beginnings to becoming a towering figure in the development of the Las Vegas Strip is a testament to his bold vision and unwavering determination. Kerkorian's impact on the city's landscape and the broader entertainment industry is a story of transformation, marked by audacious moves and a keen understanding of the dynamics of business and luxury.

Born in 1917 to Armenian immigrant parents in Fresno, California, Kerkorian's early life was steeped in adversity. The Great Depression left its mark on his family, instilling in Kerkorian a resilience and a drive to succeed that would define his career. His foray into the world of business began with a small charter flight service, which he parlayed into a larger aviation company, Trans International Airlines. This venture laid the foundation for his future successes, showcasing his ability to identify and capitalize on emerging opportunities.

Kerkorian's entry into the Las Vegas scene came in the 1960s, a time when the city was on the cusp of a transformative boom. Recognizing the potential for growth, he made his first bold move by purchasing a significant parcel of land on the Las Vegas Strip. This strategic acquisition would become the site of the iconic International Hotel, which, when it opened in 1969, was the largest hotel in the world. The success of the International Hotel was a harbinger of Kerkorian's future impact on the city's landscape.

Throughout the 1970s and 1980s, Kerkorian continued to shape the Las Vegas Strip with his visionary developments. He was the driving force behind the construction of the MGM Grand Hotel and Casino, a project that further solidified his status as a key player in the hospitality and entertainment industry. Kerkorian's approach to business was characterized by a willingness to take risks and a knack for executing large-scale projects that others might shy away from.

Kerkorian's influence extended beyond the construction of iconic hotels and casinos. He was instrumental in transforming Las Vegas into a family-friendly destination, a shift that broadened the city's appeal and fueled its growth. His strategic thinking was also evident in his ventures outside of Las Vegas, including his investments in the film industry and his attempts to acquire major automobile manufacturers.

Despite the high stakes and the intense competition, Kerkorian remained a private and enigmatic figure, shunning the spotlight and focusing on the intricacies of his deals. His legacy in Las Vegas is not just in the towering structures that bear his mark but also in the way he redefined the city as a global entertainment capital.

Kerkorian's story offers valuable lessons in strategic thinking and bold decision-making. His ability to see potential where others saw risk, his commitment to his vision, and his adaptability in the face of changing markets are principles that can be applied in various contexts. His journey from a modest background to reshaping the skyline of one of the world's most vibrant cities is a reminder that ambition, coupled with strategic acumen, can lead to extraordinary achievements.

In conclusion, Kirk Kerkorian's impact on Las Vegas is a narrative of ambition realized through strategic thinking and bold moves. His contributions to the city's development and his broader business ventures are a testament to his vision and determination. Kerkorian's story is a compelling chapter in the history of Las Vegas, offering insights into the art of the deal and the transformative power of ambition.

16 - Larry Ellison:

Larry Ellison's rise to prominence as a titan of the tech industry is a tale of relentless ambition, innovation, and strategic acumen. His journey from an adoptive background to the co-founder of Oracle Corporation is a testament to his determination to redefine the landscape of technology and business.

Born in New York City in 1944, Ellison was adopted by his aunt and uncle at a young age after contracting pneumonia. Growing up in a middle-class neighborhood in Chicago, Ellison's early life was far from the glitz and glamour of Silicon Valley. However, it was during these formative years that he developed a fierce independence and a drive to succeed, traits that would later become hallmarks of his career.

Ellison's foray into the world of technology began in the 1970s after dropping out of college twice. He moved to California, where he worked various jobs, including a stint at Amdahl Corporation, a company involved in developing IBM-compatible mainframe systems. It was here that Ellison was exposed to the burgeoning field of computer programming and the potential of relational database design.

In 1977, Ellison co-founded Software Development Laboratories (SDL) with Bob Miner and Ed Oates. The company was later renamed Oracle, inspired by a project they worked on for the Central Intelligence Agency. Oracle's big break came with the development of the first commercially available relational database, a revolutionary product that allowed users to access data in a more structured and efficient manner. This innovation propelled Oracle to the forefront of the database market, setting the stage for its dominance in the tech industry.

Ellison's drive for innovation was matched by his bold approach to business. He was known for his aggressive tactics and willingness to take risks, often entering markets dominated by larger competitors and turning the tables in Oracle's favor. His competitive spirit was not just limited to business; Ellison also made a name for himself in the world of yachting, winning the America's Cup in 2010 with his team, Oracle Team USA.

Throughout his career, Ellison's adoptive background played a significant role in shaping his approach to business and technology. His early experiences instilled in him a sense of resilience and a belief in the power of self-determination. He was not afraid to challenge the status quo or to pursue his vision, even in the face of skepticism or adversity.

Ellison's impact on the tech industry extends beyond Oracle. He has been a pivotal figure in the development of cloud computing and has made significant investments in various technology startups. His strategic thinking and ability to anticipate market trends have kept him at the forefront of technological innovation.

Larry Ellison's story is a compelling narrative of ambition, innovation, and strategic prowess in the competitive world of tech. His journey from an adoptive background to a technology mogul offers valuable lessons in perseverance, adaptability, and the relentless pursuit of excellence. Ellison's legacy in the tech industry serves as a reminder that with determination and a forward-thinking mindset, it is possible to revolutionize industries and leave an indelible mark on the world.

17 - Leonardo Del Vecchio:

Leonardo Del Vecchio's story is a testament to the power of craftsmanship, vision, and resilience. From his humble beginnings in an orphanage to becoming a titan of the eyewear industry as the founder of Luxottica, Del Vecchio's journey is a remarkable tale of a self-made industrialist who transformed adversity into opportunity.

Born in Milan, Italy, in 1935, Del Vecchio faced hardship early in life. His father passed away before he was born, and his mother, unable to provide for her five children, sent Leonardo to an orphanage. It was in this unlikely setting that Del Vecchio's journey towards greatness began. The orphanage provided him with a stable environment and access to education, instilling in him a strong work ethic and a desire to rise above his circumstances.

At the age of 14, Del Vecchio left the orphanage and began working as an apprentice to a tool and die maker in Milan. This experience was his first foray into the world of craftsmanship, and it laid the foundation for his future success. He learned the importance of precision, attention to detail, and the value of hard work. These early lessons in craftsmanship would later become the cornerstone of his business ethos.

In 1961, with a small loan and a big dream, Del Vecchio opened a small workshop in Agordo, a town in the Veneto region of Italy. The workshop specialized in making parts for eyeglasses, a niche market that was largely untapped at the time. Del Vecchio's commitment to quality and innovation quickly set his workshop apart from competitors. He introduced new manufacturing techniques and materials, such as the use of plastic for frames, which revolutionized the eyewear industry.

Del Vecchio's vision extended beyond manufacturing. He recognized the potential for eyewear to be more than just a functional item; it could be a fashion statement. In 1971, he founded Luxottica, a company that would become synonymous with luxury eyewear. Under his leadership, Luxottica acquired iconic brands such as Ray-Ban, Oakley, and Persol, and secured licensing deals with high-fashion houses like Armani, Chanel, and Prada. This strategic expansion transformed Luxottica into a global powerhouse in the eyewear industry.

Del Vecchio's humble beginnings shaped his business ethos in profound ways. He was known for his hands-on approach to leadership, often visiting factory floors and engaging with workers. His respect for craftsmanship and his belief in the dignity of labor were reflected in Luxottica's culture and operations. Del Vecchio also demonstrated a strong commitment to social responsibility, investing in community development and employee welfare.

Leonardo Del Vecchio's journey from an orphanage to eyewear mogul is a narrative of craftsmanship and vision. It highlights the importance of embracing one's roots, the value of hard work, and the power of innovation. His story serves as an inspiration to aspiring entrepreneurs and a reminder that with determination and a clear vision, it is possible to build an empire from the ground up. Del

Vecchio's legacy in the eyewear industry and his impact on the world of fashion and business are a testament to the enduring influence of a self-made industrialist.

18 - Leonid Mikhelson:

Leonid Mikhelson's ascent from the factory floor to the zenith of the energy sector is a compelling narrative of resilience, strategic acumen, and adaptability, set against the turbulent backdrop of post-Soviet Russia. His journey encapsulates the challenges of navigating the Russian business environment and his remarkable rise in the gas industry.

Born in 1955 in Kaspiysk, a small town in the Soviet Union, Mikhelson's early life was far removed from the world of business and industry. His father, an engineer, instilled in him a respect for the sciences and a strong work ethic. Mikhelson pursued a degree in industrial civil engineering from the Samara Institute of Civil Engineering, which laid the foundation for his future career in the energy sector.

Mikhelson's professional journey began on the factory floor, where he worked as a foreman for a construction company involved in building gas pipelines and infrastructure. This hands-on experience in the energy sector provided him with invaluable insights into the intricacies of the industry and the challenges of large-scale engineering projects.

The collapse of the Soviet Union in 1991 marked a turning point in Mikhelson's career and the beginning of his rise in the gas industry. The privatization of state-owned assets and the liberalization of the Russian economy presented both challenges and opportunities. Mikhelson's deep understanding of the energy sector and his strategic vision allowed him to navigate the complexities of the transitioning economy.

In 1994, Mikhelson took a bold step by acquiring a controlling stake in NOVAtek, a small gas company. Under his leadership, NOVAtek transformed from a regional player into Russia's largest independent natural gas producer. Mikhelson's strategic approach focused on investing in infrastructure, expanding production capacities, and securing long-term contracts with domestic and international customers.

One of the key challenges Mikhelson faced was the highly competitive and politically charged Russian business environment. Navigating the intricate web of political and economic interests required a delicate balance of assertiveness and diplomacy. Mikhelson's ability to forge strategic partnerships and alliances played a crucial role in NOVAtek's expansion and success.

Mikhelson's rise in the gas industry is also a testament to his commitment to innovation and sustainability. Under his leadership, NOVAtek has invested in cutting-edge technologies to improve efficiency and reduce environmental impact. The company's pioneering work in liquefied natural gas (LNG) has positioned Russia as a key player in the global LNG market.

Leonid Mikhelson's journey from the factory floor to the heights of the energy sector is a narrative that charts the challenges and triumphs of a self-made industrialist in post-Soviet Russia. His story offers valuable lessons in resilience, strategic thinking, and the importance of innovation. Mikhelson's rise in the gas industry serves as an inspiration to aspiring entrepreneurs and a reminder that with determination and a clear vision, it is possible to overcome obstacles and achieve success on a global scale.

19 - Li Ka-shing:

Li Ka-shing's odyssey from destitution to becoming a self-made global tycoon is a narrative replete with shrewdness, strategic foresight, and an unerring golden touch for investments. His journey is not merely a tale of financial acumen but also a testament to how early struggles can inform both investment strategies and philanthropic initiatives.

Born in 1928 in Chaozhou, China, Li Ka-shing's early life was fraught with hardship. His family fled to Hong Kong during the Sino-Japanese War, and by the age of 12, Li was forced to leave school and work to support his family after his father's death. These formative years were marked by poverty and toil, but they also instilled in Li a resilience and work ethic that would become the bedrock of his future success.

Li's foray into the business world began in the 1950s with a small plastics trading company. His relentless pursuit of excellence and keen eye for market trends quickly set him apart. He expanded into manufacturing, producing high-quality plastic flowers that were in demand in the post-war era. This venture laid the foundation for what would become Cheung Kong Industries, a conglomerate with interests spanning real estate, telecommunications, ports, and retail.

Li Ka-shing's investment strategies were characterized by a visionary approach and a willingness to diversify. He was not content with success in just one sector; he saw opportunities where others saw risks. His foray into the real estate market in the 1960s, at a time when Hong Kong's future was uncertain, was a gamble that paid off handsomely. Li's ability to anticipate market trends and his strategic acquisitions propelled him to become one of the leading developers in Hong Kong.

The 1970s and 1980s saw Li expanding his empire beyond Hong Kong, investing in Canada, the UK, and other parts of the world. His investments were not limited to real estate; he ventured into telecommunications, technology, and energy, always with an eye for innovation and growth potential. Li's conglomerate, Hutchison Whampoa, acquired a controlling stake in Husky Energy, marking his entry into the oil and gas industry.

Li Ka-shing's early struggles informed his investment philosophy in several ways. He valued hard work, frugality, and a long-term perspective. He was not swayed by short-term gains but focused on sustainable growth. His humble beginnings also instilled in him a sense of empathy and a desire to give back to society.

Li's philanthropic initiatives are as diverse as his business interests. Through the Li Ka Shing Foundation, he has donated billions to education, healthcare, and disaster relief. His contributions have funded universities, hospitals, and research institutes around the world. Li's philanthropy is driven by a belief in the power of education to transform lives and a commitment to improving healthcare and alleviating human suffering.

Li Ka-shing's narrative is a masterclass in strategic investment and the art of building a global empire. His journey from a struggling immigrant to a global tycoon offers valuable lessons in resilience, diversification, and the importance of giving back. Li's legacy is not just his business acumen but also his profound impact on society through his philanthropic efforts. His story is a reminder that success is not just measured by wealth, but by the positive change one can bring to the world.

20 - Madame C.J. Walker:

Madame C.J. Walker's story is an inspiring and instructional tale of entrepreneurship, self-worth, and empowerment, set against the backdrop of early 20th-century America. Born Sarah Breedlove in 1867 to formerly enslaved parents, Walker rose from the depths of poverty and discrimination to become one of the first female African American millionaires through her pioneering hair care business.

Walker's early life was marked by hardship and adversity. Orphaned at the age of seven, married at fourteen, and widowed by twenty with a young daughter, Walker's journey was one of relentless struggle. However, it was her challenges that sowed the seeds of her entrepreneurial spirit. Faced with hair loss and a lack of products suitable for African American women, Walker saw an opportunity to address a pressing need.

In the early 1900s, Walker developed a line of hair care products specifically for black women. Her products, including the "Wonderful Hair Grower," were not just about aesthetics but also about promoting scalp health and hair growth. Walker's business was revolutionary in that it provided a solution to a problem faced by countless African

American women, offering them a sense of pride and dignity in their natural beauty.

Walker's success was not solely due to her innovative products but also her savvy business acumen. She understood the power of branding and marketing, often using her image in advertisements and packaging. Walker also employed a grassroots approach, traveling across the country to demonstrate her products and train other women as sales agents. This not only expanded her business but also empowered other black women by providing them with employment opportunities and a sense of independence.

One of the most significant aspects of Walker's achievements is her role as a pioneer for female African American entrepreneurs. In an era when opportunities for black women were severely limited, Walker broke barriers and paved the way for future generations. She challenged the societal norms of her time, proving that a black woman could not only succeed in business but also become a millionaire.

Walker's impact extended beyond her business. She was a philanthropist and a vocal advocate for civil rights and women's empowerment. She used her wealth and influence to support causes she believed in, including donating to the NAACP, funding scholarships for African American students, and advocating for anti-lynching legislation.

The story of Madame C.J. Walker is a testament to the power of resilience, innovation, and determination. Her journey offers valuable lessons in entrepreneurship, self-worth, and empowerment. Walker's legacy serves as a reminder that no matter the obstacles, with vision and perseverance, one can achieve greatness and make a lasting impact on the world.

21 - Mo Ibrahim:

Mo Ibrahim's journey is a compelling narrative of innovation in technology and communications, intertwined with a strong sense of social responsibility. His contributions to the telecommunications industry in Africa through Celtel have had a profound impact on the continent's development, transforming the way people connect, do business, and access information.

Born in Sudan in 1946, Ibrahim's early life was shaped by his passion for electrical engineering. His pursuit of knowledge led him to Egypt and then to the United Kingdom, where he earned his degree and began a career that would eventually revolutionize telecommunications in Africa. Ibrahim's journey was not without challenges, but his resilience and determination propelled him forward.

In the mid-1990s, Ibrahim recognized the transformative potential of mobile telecommunications in Africa, a continent where the vast distances and lack of infrastructure made traditional communication methods inadequate. In 1998, he founded Celtel, a mobile phone company that would go on to provide services to millions of people across Africa. Celtel's success was not just in its ability to provide connectivity but also in its innovative business model, which focused on transparency, good governance, and social responsibility.

Celtel's entry into the African market marked a turning point in the continent's telecommunications landscape. Prior to Celtel, mobile phone services were limited and expensive, making them inaccessible to the majority of the population. Celtel's affordable and reliable services bridged this gap, enabling people in even the most remote areas to connect with the rest of the world. This connectivity had far-reaching implications for economic development, education, healthcare, and social cohesion.

One of the most significant impacts of Celtel's work was its contribution to economic development. The availability of mobile communication services opened up new opportunities for commerce, allowing businesses to operate more efficiently and access wider markets. It also facilitated financial inclusion through mobile banking, empowering individuals and communities previously excluded from the formal financial system.

Ibrahim's vision extended beyond the commercial success of Celtel. He was deeply committed to the principles of good governance and ethical business practices. Under his leadership, Celtel became known for its transparency and anti-corruption policies, setting a standard for corporate governance in Africa. This commitment to ethical business practices earned Celtel the trust of its customers and respect from the international community.

Beyond his achievements in telecommunications, Mo Ibrahim has been a vocal advocate for good governance and leadership in Africa. After selling Celtel in 2005, he established the Mo Ibrahim Foundation, which promotes good governance and leadership on the continent through the Ibrahim Index of African Governance and the Ibrahim Prize for Achievement in African Leadership. These initiatives reflect Ibrahim's belief in the importance of accountable and effective leadership for Africa's development.

Mo Ibrahim's story is a testament to the power of technology and communications to drive social and economic progress. His work with Celtel and his ongoing efforts to promote good governance in Africa highlight the role of innovation and ethical leadership in creating a more connected and equitable world. Ibrahim's legacy serves as an inspiration to entrepreneurs and leaders everywhere, demonstrating that business success and social responsibility can go hand in hand.

22 - Oprah Winfrey:

Oprah Winfrey's journey is an emotionally intelligent narrative that masterfully intertwines personal struggle with an unparalleled ability to connect with and influence millions. Born into poverty in rural Mississippi in 1954, Winfrey's early life was marked by hardship, including sexual abuse and teenage pregnancy. Despite these challenges, she rose to become one of the most influential media personalities and philanthropists in the world.

Winfrey's childhood was a time of both adversity and resilience. Raised by her grandmother, she learned to read at an early age, and her love for storytelling and communication began to blossom. However, her move to Milwaukee to live with her mother introduced her to a harsher reality, where she faced abuse and neglect. These early experiences of trauma and struggle would later become a source of strength and empathy, allowing her to connect deeply with others who had similar experiences.

After moving to Nashville to live with her father, Winfrey's life began to transform. Her father's strict discipline and emphasis on education helped her to excel in school and win a scholarship to Tennessee State University. It was during this time that Winfrey's career in media began, as she became the first African American female news anchor at Nashville's WLAC-TV.

Winfrey's move to Chicago in 1984 to host the morning talk show "AM Chicago" marked a turning point in her career. She transformed the show into "The Oprah Winfrey Show," which quickly became a national sensation. Her emotional intelligence, authenticity, and ability to connect with her audience set her apart. Winfrey's show tackled difficult topics, from addiction and mental health to racism and poverty, with a level of empathy and understanding that resonated with viewers.

Winfrey's personal struggles informed her approach to her media career. She used her platform to give a voice to the voiceless and to create a space for healing and open dialogue. Her ability to share her own vulnerabilities and to listen deeply to others' stories fostered a sense of community and empathy among her audience.

Beyond her media empire, Winfrey's influence extends to her philanthropic efforts. She has used her wealth and platform to support various causes, including education, women's empowerment, and disaster relief. Her establishment of the Oprah Winfrey Leadership Academy for Girls in South Africa is a testament to her commitment to empowering young women and providing them with opportunities to succeed.

Winfrey's journey from a troubled childhood to a global icon is a powerful example of the impact of personal struggles on one's ability to connect with and influence others. Her emotional intelligence, resilience, and generosity have made her not only a media mogul but also a beacon of hope and inspiration for millions. Oprah Winfrey's story teaches us that our greatest challenges can become our greatest sources of strength, and that empathy and understanding can pave the way for profound change and connection.

23 - Ralph Lauren:

Ralph Lauren's journey from the humble beginnings in the Bronx to the pinnacle of American fashion is a narrative steeped in a keen eye for detail and an unwavering commitment to classic Americana style. Born Ralph Lifshitz in 1939 to Jewish immigrant parents, Lauren's early life was far removed from the glitz and glamour of the fashion world. Yet, it was in the streets of the Bronx that he cultivated his unique vision of style, one that would eventually redefine American fashion.

Growing up, Lauren was captivated by the allure of cinema and the impeccable style of movie stars. This fascination with the elegance and grace of Hollywood's golden era planted the seeds for his future in fashion. Despite his modest upbringing, Lauren possessed a natural flair for style, often saving his money to buy suits that would set him apart from his peers.

Lauren's foray into the fashion industry began not with designing clothes but with selling ties. In 1967, while working as a sales assistant at Brooks Brothers, he launched a line of wide, hand-made ties under the label "Polo." His ties, with their bold colors and patterns, were a departure from the conventional styles of the time and quickly caught the attention of major department stores. This early success was a turning point for Lauren, marking the beginning of his journey to build a global fashion empire.

The launch of Polo by Ralph Lauren in 1968 marked the expansion of his brand into a full menswear line. Lauren's designs were characterized by their classic, timeless style, drawing inspiration from the American West, the preppy look of the Ivy League, and the sophistication of English nobility. His ability to blend these diverse influences into a cohesive aesthetic set him apart in the fashion industry.

Lauren's vision for his brand was not just about clothes; it was about creating a lifestyle. He was among the first designers to open a flagship store, the Polo Shop on Rodeo Drive in Beverly Hills, which offered customers an immersive experience into the world of Ralph Lauren. His advertisements, often featuring models in picturesque settings, further reinforced the aspirational lifestyle his brand represented.

The expansion of Ralph Lauren into women's wear, home furnishings, and fragrances solidified its status as a lifestyle brand. Lauren's keen eye for detail and his commitment to quality were evident in every product that bore his name. His designs were not just clothes; they were embodiments of a refined, classic American style that appealed to a wide audience.

Lauren's humble beginnings in the Bronx were a constant source of inspiration for his brand. He often spoke of his admiration for the American dream and his desire to create a brand that embodied its ideals. His success story is a testament to the power of vision, determination, and the ability to turn dreams into reality.

Ralph Lauren's journey from a young boy in the Bronx to a titan of American fashion is a narrative of classic Americana style, marked by a keen eye for detail and an unwavering dedication to his vision. His story serves as an inspiration to aspiring designers and entrepreneurs, reminding us that with passion, creativity, and hard work, it is possible to leave an indelible mark on the world.

24 - Richard Branson:

Richard Branson's journey to becoming a billionaire is a captivating narrative that combines adventure, innovation, and a touch of eccentricity, reflecting his bold and unconventional approach to business and life. Born in 1950 in Surrey, England, Branson's early struggles with dyslexia and poor academic performance did not dampen his entrepreneurial spirit. Instead, they fueled his determination to carve his own path.

Branson's foray into the business world began in the late 1960s with the launch of Student, a magazine aimed at young people. Despite the magazine's modest success, it was the mail-order record business he started from the magazine's office that laid the foundation for his future empire. This venture, named Virgin, was Branson's first major business breakthrough, offering discounted records and challenging established retailers.

The success of the mail-order business led to the opening of the first Virgin Records store in London in 1971. The store became a popular hangout for music lovers, and its success prompted Branson to take a bold step into the music industry. In 1972, he launched Virgin Records, the record label that would become synonymous with groundbreaking artists like Mike Oldfield, whose album "Tubular Bells" became a sensation, and later, iconic bands like the Sex Pistols.

Branson's entrepreneurial journey was marked by a series of daring adventures and groundbreaking ideas. In 1984, he entered the aviation industry with the launch of Virgin Atlantic, challenging established airlines with a focus on customer service and innovation. His foray into space tourism with Virgin Galactic further exemplified his willingness to push boundaries and explore new frontiers.

Throughout his career, Branson has been known for his adventurous spirit and willingness to take risks. His attempts to break world records, including crossing the Atlantic Ocean in a hot air balloon, have become legendary. These daring escapades not only captured the public's imagination but also embodied Branson's philosophy of living life to the fullest and embracing the unknown.

Branson's journey has not been without its challenges. He has faced numerous setbacks, including business failures and near-death experiences during his record-breaking attempts. However, his resilience and ability to bounce back from adversity have been key to his success. He has often spoken about the importance of learning from failures and using them as stepping stones to success.

In addition to his business achievements, Branson is also known for his philanthropic efforts and commitment to social causes. Through the Virgin Group and his foundation, Virgin Unite, he has championed various initiatives focused on environmental sustainability, healthcare, and education.

Richard Branson's story is a testament to the power of thinking differently, embracing challenges, and pursuing one's passions with relentless enthusiasm. His journey from a dyslexic schoolboy to a billionaire entrepreneur is a source of inspiration for aspiring entrepreneurs and adventurers alike. It serves as a reminder that with creativity, courage, and a touch of eccentricity, it is possible to turn dreams into reality and leave a lasting impact on the world.

25 - Roman Abramovich:

Roman Abramovich's story is a remarkable narrative of resilience and adaptability, set against the backdrop of the geopolitical changes in Eastern Europe. Born in 1966 in Saratov, Russia, Abramovich was orphaned at a young age and raised by relatives in the harsh industrial city of Ukhta in the Komi Republic. Despite these early life challenges, he would rise to become one of Russia's most influential businessmen and a global figure in the world of football.

Abramovich's journey to success began in the tumultuous years following the collapse of the Soviet Union. The rapid privatization of state assets and the emergence of a market economy provided unprecedented opportunities for those with the acumen and audacity to seize them. Abramovich, with his keen instincts and entrepreneurial spirit, was among those who navigated the chaotic landscape of post-Soviet Russia to amass considerable wealth.

In the early 1990s, Abramovich ventured into the oil industry, acquiring stakes in the newly privatized oil companies. His most significant move came in 1995 when he and his partners acquired a controlling interest in the giant oil company Sibneft through a controversial loans-for-shares program. The consolidation of Sibneft under Abramovich's control marked his ascent to the ranks of Russia's oligarchs.

Abramovich's rise was not only a testament to his business acumen but also his ability to adapt to the shifting political and economic currents of post-Soviet Russia. He cultivated relationships with influential figures in the Kremlin, ensuring that his business interests were aligned with the prevailing political winds. This adaptability was crucial in a country where the lines between business and politics were often blurred.

In 2003, Abramovich made a move that would catapult him onto the global stage. He acquired the English football club Chelsea FC, transforming it into one of the most successful clubs in the world. His investment in Chelsea was not just a business venture but also a statement of his ambitions on the global stage. Under his ownership, Chelsea won numerous domestic and international titles, becoming a powerhouse in European football.

Abramovich's impact on Russian business and global football is undeniable. In Russia, he is seen as a symbol of the country's transition from a planned economy to a market-driven one, albeit with all the complexities and controversies that come with such a transformation. In the world of football, he is credited with changing the business dynamics of the sport, ushering in an era of billionaire club owners who are willing to invest vast sums of money to secure success.

However, Abramovich's story is also a reflection of the challenges faced by those who rose to prominence in the post-Soviet era. His business dealings have been scrutinized and criticized, and he has had to navigate the complexities of international sanctions and geopolitical tensions.

Roman Abramovich's journey from an orphan in the Soviet Union to a billionaire businessman and influential figure in global football is a narrative of resilience and adaptability. It is a story that offers insights into the rapid changes that have shaped Eastern Europe and the global business landscape in recent decades. His life serves as a reminder of the opportunities and challenges that come with periods of profound transformation.

26 - Sam Walton:

Sam Walton's story is a no-nonsense, practical narrative about retail and the value of understanding your customer. His journey from a small-town store owner to the founder of Walmart, the world's largest retailer, is a testament to his innovative approaches to retail and the impact of his small-town values on the company's corporate culture.

Born in 1918 in Kingfisher, Oklahoma, Walton grew up during the Great Depression. These early years instilled in him a sense of frugality and an understanding of the challenges faced by ordinary people. After serving in World War II, Walton took his first steps into the retail world by purchasing a Ben Franklin variety store in Newport, Arkansas, in 1945. This experience laid the foundation for his retail philosophy, centered on offering low prices and great value.

Walton's breakthrough came in 1962 when he opened the first Walmart store in Rogers, Arkansas. His vision was simple yet revolutionary: to offer customers a wide range of goods at the lowest possible prices in a friendly, welcoming environment. Walton's approach was rooted in his belief in the power of volume selling. By keeping prices low and focusing on high sales volume, he could generate significant profits while passing savings onto the customer.

One of Walton's most innovative retail strategies was his focus on rural markets. While other retailers concentrated on urban areas, Walton saw an opportunity in serving small-town America. He believed that by bringing low prices and a wide selection to these underserved areas, he could tap into a vast market. This strategy not only fueled Walmart's growth but also transformed the retail landscape.

Walton's small-town values were at the heart of Walmart's corporate culture. He fostered a sense of community and family among his employees, whom he referred to as "associates." Walton believed in leading by example, often visiting stores to meet with associates and customers, and listening to their feedback. This hands-on approach helped him stay connected to the needs of his customers and maintain the company's focus on customer service.

Another key aspect of Walton's retail philosophy was his commitment to continuous improvement and innovation. He was a firm believer in the power of technology to enhance efficiency and reduce costs. Walmart was an early adopter of barcoding and computerized inventory systems, which allowed the company to manage its vast supply chain more effectively and keep prices low.

Walton's impact on the retail industry is immeasurable. His approach to low-cost retailing and focus on customer satisfaction revolutionized the way goods are sold and set new standards for the industry. Under his leadership, Walmart grew from a single store to a global retail giant, changing the face of retail and becoming a model for other companies to follow.

Sam Walton's story is a powerful reminder of the importance of understanding your customer and staying true to your values. His innovative approaches to retail, combined with his small-town values, shaped Walmart's corporate culture and paved the way for its success. Walton's legacy lives on in the company he built and the principles he instilled, serving as an inspiration for entrepreneurs and business leaders around the world.

27 - Shahid Khan:

Shahid Khan's story is a determined and hopeful narrative of an immigrant realizing the American industrial dream. His journey from a dishwasher to an automotive tycoon, and his contributions to American football and English soccer, exemplify the possibilities that come with hard work, vision, and perseverance.

Born in 1950 in Lahore, Pakistan, Khan's early life was marked by a desire for greater opportunities. In 1967, at the age of 16, he took a bold step toward realizing his dreams by moving to the United States to study engineering at the University of Illinois at Urbana-Champaign. Arriving with just a few dollars in his pocket, Khan's initial days in America were challenging. He took up a job as a dishwasher, earning $1.20 an hour, to support himself through college.

Khan's first foray into the automotive industry came after his graduation when he started working at the automotive manufacturing company Flex-N-Gate. His engineering background and innovative mindset led him to develop a revolutionary one-piece truck bumper, a design that would set a new standard in the industry. In 1980, seizing the opportunity to control his destiny, Khan bought Flex-N-Gate from his former employer, embarking on a journey to transform it into a global powerhouse.

Under Khan's leadership, Flex-N-Gate experienced phenomenal growth, expanding its operations worldwide and becoming a leading supplier to major automakers. Khan's success in the automotive industry is a testament to his entrepreneurial spirit, his ability to innovate, and his commitment to quality and efficiency.

Khan's achievements extend beyond the automotive industry. In 2011, he made headlines by becoming the first member of an ethnic minority to own an NFL team, the Jacksonville Jaguars. His acquisition of the team was a historic moment in American sports and a reflection of Khan's passion for football and his belief in the power of sports to unite people.

In 2013, Khan further expanded his presence in the sports world by purchasing the English soccer club Fulham FC. His investment in Fulham FC demonstrated his commitment to nurturing talent and his vision for building successful sports franchises that resonate with fans and communities.

Khan's journey from a dishwasher to a billionaire is a powerful embodiment of the American dream. It is a story of determination, hope, and the relentless pursuit of success. His contributions to the automotive industry, American football, and English soccer are a testament to his diverse interests and his ability to excel in various fields.

Shahid Khan's story offers valuable lessons in resilience, innovation, and the importance of staying true to one's vision. His life serves as an inspiration to immigrants and aspiring entrepreneurs, reminding us that with hard work and determination, anything is possible.

28 - Soichiro Honda:

Soichiro Honda's story is a visionary and inventive narrative of post-war recovery and industrial triumph in the automotive world. Born in 1906 in a small village in Japan, Honda's journey from a humble mechanic to the founder of one of the world's leading automobile manufacturers is a testament to his persistence, innovative spirit, and unyielding dedication to his dreams.

Honda's early life was marked by a passion for mechanics and a keen interest in automobiles. Despite facing financial difficulties, he pursued his interests with relentless determination. He started his career as a mechanic, eventually opening his own auto repair shop. However, it was his foray into the manufacturing of piston rings that marked the beginning of his journey into the automotive industry. Despite initial failures and the rejection of his piston rings by Toyota, Honda's unwavering commitment to quality and improvement eventually led to success.

The turning point in Honda's career came after World War II when Japan faced severe fuel shortages. Honda's innovative spirit shone through as he developed a motorized bicycle powered by a small engine. This invention was not only a solution to the fuel crisis but also marked the birth of Honda Motor Co., Ltd. in 1948. The company's first motorcycle, the Honda Cub, became a symbol of post-war recovery and resilience, transforming the way people moved around in Japan.

Honda's philosophy of innovation was evident in his approach to the automotive industry. He believed in the power of dreams and the importance of challenging the status quo. Under his leadership, Honda Motor Co., Ltd. became known for its cutting-edge technology, high-quality products, and environmental consciousness. The company's entry into the automobile market with the Honda T360 mini truck and the S500 sports car showcased Honda's commitment to diversifying and pushing the boundaries of automotive design and engineering.

One of Honda's most significant contributions to the automotive industry was his emphasis on research and development. He established the Honda Technical Research Institute, which became a hub for innovation and the development of new technologies. Honda's dedication to innovation led to numerous breakthroughs, including the development of the CVCC engine, which significantly reduced emissions and set new standards for environmental responsibility in the automotive industry.

Honda's persistence in overcoming early failures and his philosophy of innovation were not just limited to his professional life. He was known for his dynamic personality, his love for racing, and his belief in the power of competition to drive progress. Honda's involvement in motorsports, including Formula One, was driven by his desire to test the limits of his machines and to continuously improve their performance.

Soichiro Honda's story is a remarkable narrative of overcoming adversity, embracing innovation, and achieving industrial triumph in the post-war era. His legacy lives on in the Honda Motor Co., Ltd., which continues to be a global leader in the automotive industry. Honda's journey from a small repair shop to a multinational corporation serves as an inspiration to entrepreneurs and innovators worldwide, reminding us that with persistence, vision, and a willingness to challenge the conventional, it is possible to achieve extraordinary success.

29 - Ursula Burns:

Ursula Burns' story is a trailblazing narrative that underscores tenacity and leadership in corporate America. Her rise from a low-income neighborhood in New York City to become the first African American woman CEO of a Fortune 500 company, Xerox Corporation, is a testament to her determination, intelligence, and commitment to breaking barriers.

Born in 1958, Burns grew up in a housing project on Manhattan's Lower East Side. Her mother, a Panamanian immigrant, worked multiple jobs to support Burns and her siblings, instilling in them the importance of education and hard work. Despite the challenges of her environment, Burns excelled academically, earning a scholarship to attend an all-girls Catholic high school and later graduating with a degree in mechanical engineering from the Polytechnic Institute of NYU.

Burns' career at Xerox began in 1980 as a summer intern. Her talent and work ethic quickly set her apart, and she rose through the ranks, holding various engineering and management positions. In the mid-1990s, Burns led several of Xerox's business teams, including the office color and fax business and office network printing business. Her leadership in these roles was marked by her ability to drive innovation and efficiency, significantly contributing to the company's growth.

In 2009, Burns made history when she was named CEO of Xerox, becoming the first African American woman to lead a Fortune 500 company. Under her leadership, Xerox underwent a significant transformation, shifting from a focus on traditional printing to becoming a leader in business process and document management services. Burns' vision for the company was to adapt to the changing technological landscape and to position Xerox as a services-led, technology-driven company.

Burns' tenure as CEO was not without challenges. She faced the task of navigating the company through the global financial crisis and the rapidly evolving tech industry. However, her strategic acumen, focus on innovation, and commitment to sustainability and diversity helped Xerox remain a competitive force in the market.

Beyond her achievements at Xerox, Burns has been a vocal advocate for diversity and inclusion in corporate America. She has served on various boards, including the Obama administration's President's Export Council and the board of directors for Uber, and has been a mentor and role model for aspiring leaders, particularly women and people of color.

Ursula Burns' journey from a low-income neighborhood to the pinnacle of corporate America is a reflection of her indomitable spirit and leadership prowess. Her story is a powerful reminder that with tenacity, hard work, and a commitment to excellence, it is possible to overcome obstacles and achieve greatness. Burns' legacy extends beyond her accomplishments at Xerox, serving as an inspiration for future generations of leaders striving to make their mark in the business world.

30 - Wally Amos:

Wally Amos' story is a warm and engaging narrative about the power of personality, the sweet taste of success, and the resilience required to overcome business challenges. His journey from a humble beginning to the founder of the famous cookie brand, Famous Amos, is a testament to his infectious enthusiasm, unwavering determination, and innovative spirit.

Born in 1936 in Tallahassee, Florida, Amos faced early life challenges, including his parents' separation when he was just two years old. He moved to New York City to live with his aunt, where he developed a love for baking, a skill he learned from his aunt. Despite the difficulties of his early years, Amos' charismatic personality and positive outlook on life shone through.

Amos' career began in the entertainment industry, where he worked as a talent agent at the William Morris Agency. He represented big names like Simon & Garfunkel and Marvin Gaye. However, it was his homemade chocolate chip cookies, which he often shared with his clients, that eventually stole the spotlight. Encouraged by friends and clients, Amos turned his passion for baking into a business venture.

In 1975, Amos opened the first Famous Amos cookie store in Los Angeles, California. His cookies quickly gained popularity, not only for their delicious taste but also for Amos' charismatic marketing approach. He became the smiling face of the brand, often seen wearing his signature straw hat and embroidered shirt. Amos' personal touch and the homey feel of his stores resonated with customers, turning Famous Amos into a beloved brand.

However, Amos' journey was not without its challenges. As the company expanded, he faced financial difficulties and eventually lost control of the Famous Amos brand in the 1980s. Despite this setback, Amos' resilience and positive spirit remained unshaken. He continued to pursue his passion for baking and entrepreneurship, launching new ventures such as Uncle Wally's Muffin Company.

Amos' story is a lesson in the power of personality and the importance of staying true to oneself. His ability to connect with people and his genuine love for what he did were key factors in his success. Even in the face of business challenges, Amos maintained his optimism and continued to spread joy through his baking.

In addition to his entrepreneurial endeavors, Amos has been an advocate for literacy and education. He founded the Read It Loud! Foundation, encouraging parents to read aloud to their children. His commitment to making a positive impact extends beyond his business achievements, showcasing his dedication to giving back to the community.

Wally Amos' journey from a simple cookie recipe to a beloved brand is a heartwarming tale of success, resilience, and the enduring power of a warm personality. His story inspires aspiring entrepreneurs to pursue their passions, stay true to their values, and face challenges with a positive attitude. Through his cookies and his charitable work, Amos has left an indelible mark on the world, proving that sometimes, the sweetest successes come from the simplest beginnings.

~ ~ ~ ~ ~

Epilogue

As these tales draw to a close, let us not forget that they are but the prelude to the most important story yet to be told—yours. You have journeyed through the lives of those who have climbed from depths to pinnacles, who have transformed scarcity into abundance and adversity into opportunity. Now, the torch is passed to you, not just to carry but to ignite the path ahead.

Consider this not an end, but an invitation. An invitation to cast aside the cloak of doubt and wear resilience as your mantle. An invitation to step into the arena where challenge beckons and to carve a path that others will follow. The world is abundant with possibility, yet it yearns for the spark of your unique contribution.

So rise, creators of tomorrow. Rise with the knowledge that the foundations of greatness are often laid with the bricks of hardship. Rise with the understanding that your potential is a sleeping giant awaiting your call. Step forth from the shadows of contemplation into the light of action. Build, innovate, lead, and above all, transform the fervor of your dreams into the blueprint of reality.

May you find the courage to start, the strength to endure, and the resolve to finish. May your actions resonate with the echo of these stories, and may your journey be a testament to the indomitable human spirit. Your time is not just coming—it is now, it is here. Seize it.

~ ~ ~ ~ ~

~ ~ ~ ~ ~

~ ~ ~ ~ ~

Dedication

This book is dedicated to the dreamers, the doers, and the believers who dare to turn their visions into reality. May the stories within these pages inspire you to embrace your journey, overcome obstacles, and savor the sweet taste of success.

Always grateful,

Kevin James Joseph McNamara

~ ~

#KevinJamesJosephMcNamara
#KevinJJosephMcNamara
#KevinJJMcNamara

From Broke to Billionaire